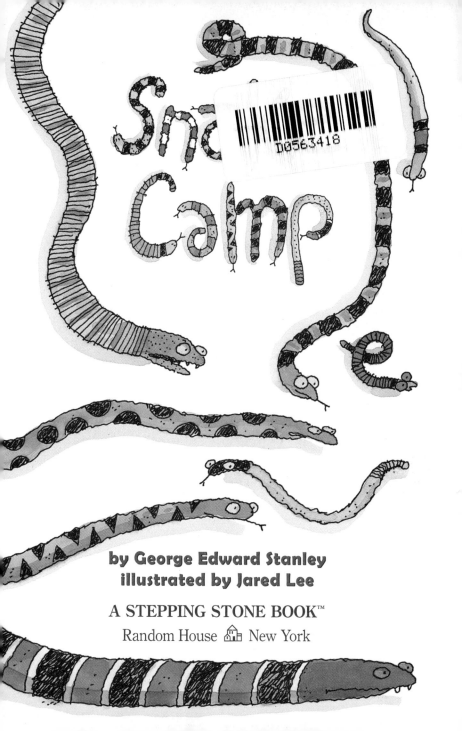

Snake Camp

by George Edward Stanley
illustrated by Jared Lee

A STEPPING STONE BOOK™

Random House New York

*For Jen—for more reasons than I could possibly
list on one page, and, as always, for Gwen,
Charles, James, and Tambye, with all my love
—G.E.S.*

*To Morgan Greer, Miss Hollywood
—J.L.*

Text copyright © 2000 by George Edward Stanley. Illustrations copyright © 2000
by Jared Lee. All rights reserved under International and Pan-American Copyright
Conventions. Published in the United States by Random House Children's Books,
a division of Random House, Inc., New York, and simultaneously in Canada by
Random House of Canada Limited, Toronto. Originally published by Golden
Books, an imprint of Random House Children's Books, a division of Random
House, Inc., New York, in 2000.

www.randomhouse.com/kids

Library of Congress Cataloging-in-Publication Data
Stanley, George Edward.
Snake camp / by George Edward Stanley ; illustrated by Jared Lee. —
1st Random House ed.
    p. cm. "A Stepping Stone Book."
SUMMARY: When Stevie Marsh leaves for his stay at Camp Viper, he believes
it is a camp to learn about "Viper" computer software.
ISBN 0-307-26406-8 (pbk.) — ISBN 0-307-46406-7 (lib. bdg.)
[1. Snakes—Fiction. 2. Camps—Fiction.] I. Lee, Jared D., ill. II. Title.
PZ7.S78694Sn 2003 [Fic]—dc21 2002153691

First Random House Edition
Printed in the United States of America   17 16 15 14 13 12 11 10 9 8

Contents

Ophiolium

1
CAMP VIPER

Stevie Marsh stared out the window of the bright green Camp Viper bus. He waved to his parents one last time.

"Be sure to write Mommy and Daddy every day, Stevie!" his mother called.

The other campers started to giggle. Stevie quickly turned away.

Why couldn't his mother just cry like the other mothers? Why did she have to say stuff like that?

When he looked out the window again, he saw his father pointing to his watch. Stevie knew what that meant. If they didn't hurry up and leave now, his father would be late to teach his Latin class at the university.

Stevie slumped against the seat and let out a big sigh. Sure he wanted to learn about "Viper" computer software. But why did he have to do it at camp? Why couldn't he just learn at home?

Stevie had never been to camp before.

But he knew he wouldn't like it there. Camps were in the woods. And the woods were full of bugs and poison ivy and *snakes*.

Stevie shivered. He didn't like snakes at all.

A boy with bright red hair sat down beside him as the bus pulled away from the curb. "Hi. I'm Jordan Jacoby," the boy said. "What's your name?"

"Stevie Marsh."

"I don't remember you from last year," said Jordan. "Is this your first trip to Camp Viper?"

Stevie nodded.

"You're going to love it," Jordan said.

Stevie tried to smile. "Do they have a lot of really neat computers there?"

Jordan looked puzzled. "I think they've got a couple." He grinned. "But why would you want to play with computers when they've got all those great snakes?"

Stevie gulped. Snakes?

Jordan went on. "Camp Viper is the best place in the whole world to learn about snakes."

Snakes! Oh, no! "Viper" was the name of a brand-new software program. But now Stevie remembered that a viper was also a type of snake.

His parents must have made a mistake. He wasn't going to computer camp! He was going to . . .

SNAKE CAMP!

2
PICKING A SNAKE

The bus turned off the highway and onto a narrow dirt road. It stopped in a clearing.

"We're here!" said Jordan excitedly. "Look, Stevie! There's the Ophiolium."

"The what?" Stevie asked.

"The Ophiolium. The place where they keep the snakes," said Jordan.

Stevie looked. The Ophiolium was big. Too big. He imagined thousands of snakes—all in one huge pile.

"That's the Main Lodge." Jordan pointed to another building.

Stevie gasped. The front door was carved to look like the mouth of a huge snake!

Jordan stood up. "Come on!" he said. "Let's go!"

Stevie slowly followed Jordan off the bus and through the creepy snake's mouth.

Inside, one of the counselors was writing on a clipboard.

"Hi, Tim!" said Jordan.

"Hi, Jordan! Welcome back!" Tim said. "This year try not to pick a *biting* snake." He chuckled.

Jordan laughed, too.

Stevie felt like he was going to pass out.

Jordan nodded at Stevie. "He's new."

"Then let's put you two together," said Tim. He checked his clipboard. "You'll be in Cabin Rattlesnake. It's right next door. Okay?"

"Okay!" Jordan said.

Tim looked at his watch. "Go take your suitcases to the cabin. Then head

on over to the Ophiolium. It's about
time to pick a snake for the summer."

Stevie jumped. "Pick a snake?"

Jordan nodded. "Yeah! Come on!
The best ones go fast."

Stevie had to get out now. It was his
only chance! He'd hide on the bus and

ride back to the city when it left.

"Oh! I just remembered," he said. "I left something on the bus!"

Jordan gave him a suspicious look. "You can get it later," he said. "The bus stays here all summer."

Stevie saw his chance disappear. "I'll get it anyway and meet you at the Ophiolium," he mumbled.

Stevie walked to the bus and sat down next to one of the big tires. He put his head on his suitcase. What was he going to do? How could he spend a summer surrounded by snakes?

Suddenly, he had an idea. A great

idea! He opened his suitcase, grabbed a shoe box, and dumped out the shoes.

He punched some air holes in the box and wrote DO NOT OPEN in big letters on it.

Then he raced to the Ophiolium.

Jordan was waiting for him outside. "What's in the box?" he asked.

"It's my snake," Stevie replied. "I thought we were supposed to bring our own."

Now Jordan looked even more suspicious. Stevie pretended not to notice. Together they went inside the Ophiolium.

Everywhere Stevie looked, he saw
snakes. They were all hissing. They
looked slimy and scaly and scary.

One by one, each camper chose a
snake. Tim, the Head Counselor, called
out the snake's name. Eastern Hognose
Snake. Western Shovelnose Snake.

Mexican Hooknose Snake. Northern
Black Racer.

Stevie didn't know there were so
many types of snakes.

Jordan picked a Black Swamp
Snake. "This guy reminds me of
Ralph," he whispered to Stevie as the

snake wrapped itself around his wrist.

"Ralph?" Stevie asked.

"My pet bullsnake," Jordan explained. "He sleeps with me and everything." Stevie shuddered.

Then it was his turn.

"I don't need to choose a snake," Stevie told Tim. He held up his box. "I brought my own."

Tim looked puzzled. "Oh. What kind of snake is it?"

Stevie tried to remember some of the Latin words his father used at home.

Finally, he whispered, "Horribilis Slimus Vipera."

"What?" Tim asked.

"HORRIBILIS SLIMUS VIPERA!"
Stevie shouted.

"I've never heard of that snake,"
said Tim. "Would you show it to us?"

Stevie shook his head. "It's allergic to
light. It only comes out when the sun
and moon are hidden by dark clouds."

Tim narrowed his eyes.

Stevie held his breath. Would Tim tell everyone that he was making this up? Would the other campers laugh at him?

Instead, Tim put his arm around Stevie's shoulders. "This is so exciting, campers!" he said. "If it rains a lot this summer, you'll get to see one of the rarest snakes in the world."

Everyone clapped.

What am I going to do now? Stevie wondered. *What will happen when everyone finds out I'm holding an empty box?*

3
SLIME JELLO

A couple of nights later, Stevie was lying in bed, trying to fall asleep.

Jordan was reading with a flashlight. Suddenly, he whispered, "Stevie! I think your snake is a phony!"

Stevie sat up. "It is not!" Everyone else had bought his snake story. But Jordan was still suspicious.

"There's no Horribilis Slimus Vipera listed in my *Encyclopedia of Snakes*," Jordan whispered. "And this book has the name of every snake in the world."

"They must have discovered it after they wrote that book," Stevie said. "Because this snake is real!"

"No, it's not!" Jordan shouted.

Several kids yelled, "Be quiet!"

"Yeah, Jordan. You're making it nervous," Stevie whispered. He kept the box under the covers, so Jordan couldn't open it after he went to sleep. "I can feel it moving around inside."

"I hope it rains tomorrow," Jordan

said. "You'll have to show me then."

After a few minutes, Stevie heard Jordan snoring. But there was no way he could sleep now. He had to do something. Once and for all he had to convince Jordan that there really was a snake in that box. But how?

Stevie's stomach rumbled. He hadn't eaten much at dinner. After all, his favorite meal was definitely not liverwurst sandwiches and lime jello.

Lime jello! That was the answer!

Stevie slipped out of bed. He took Jordan's flashlight and headed to the Dining Hall.

Stevie found what he wanted in the refrigerator. A big bowl of lime jello. He grabbed it and hurried back to the cabin.

He crept quietly to Jordan's bed and poured the jello all over him.

Then Stevie got back into bed.

Jordan's screaming woke him the next morning.

"What's wrong?" Stevie asked.

"Look at me!" Jordan whimpered.

"Oh, no!" Stevie cried. He jumped out of bed and stood beside Jordan. The rest of the kids in the cabin gathered around them.

"Yuck!" they were all saying. "What is that stuff?"

"It's green slime," Stevie said. "My snake did it."

Everyone backed away.

"What do you mean?" Jordan croaked.

"That's why it's called Horribilis

Slimus Vipera," Stevie explained. "It leaves green slime everywhere it crawls."

Jordan's eyes got huge.

"My snake woke me during the night. The moon must have been covered by clouds. It senses that, you know," Stevie told them. "So I let it out to look for food. But I didn't realize it was crawling all over Jordan. I'm sorry."

A couple of the kids helped Jordan to the showers. Stevie stayed where he was. He pretended to talk to his snake.

Finally, everyone went to breakfast. Stevie was alone in the cabin.

He put the box down and leaned against his bunk. He'd only been at camp a few days. How could he keep this up for another three weeks? Sooner or later, someone would discover the truth.

Maybe he should just go to bed and not get up until the last day of camp.

Suddenly, Stevie had a funny feeling—like he was being watched. He looked to his left. Two black eyes were staring at him.

"Yikes!" he cried.

It was a snake.

4
EMERALD

Stevie screamed.

The snake tilted its head.

Stevie screamed again.

The snake flicked its tongue.

Stevie screamed one more time. He was shaking all over. His heart was pounding.

But the snake just sat there.

Stevie looked at it more closely. The snake didn't look slimy. Of course, it *was* green. So how could you tell?

There was only one way to find out.

Stevie reached out slowly and touched the snake on its back. The snake didn't feel slimy at all!

And it didn't seem to mind being touched. In fact, it even looked kind of friendly.

Stevie realized that he had stopped shaking. And his heart wasn't pounding anymore, either.

He was still nervous. But he was no longer afraid of this snake!

Stevie knew exactly what he had to do. He closed his eyes for a second. He took a deep breath. Then he slowly picked up the snake and put it inside the box.

He had a real snake! And he could hardly wait to tell Jordan. He ran to the Dining Hall.

"Why'd you bring that slimy thing in here?" Jordan demanded.

"This isn't the Horribilis Slimus Vipera," Stevie said. "I put it inside my . . . my suitcase."

"Your suitcase?"

"Yeah, my suitcase," Stevie said lamely.

Jordan blinked. "Oh. What's in the box now?"

Stevie opened it. "I'm going to study this snake instead."

Jordan laughed. "Stevie! That's a Smooth Green Snake. Nobody studies them. They're too common."

"Not to me. I only know about rare snakes, remember? The Horribilis Slimus Vipera is the rarest snake in the world."

That made sense to Jordan.

Now Stevie had a snake to study just like all the other campers.

That afternoon, Stevie started learning about the Smooth Green Snake. And Jordan even helped.

"Smooth Green Snakes live all over this area," Jordan told him. "They like grassy places. But you can find them in bushes and vines, too."

Stevie named his snake Rocky. But

two days later the snake laid some
eggs. So Stevie changed her name to
Emerald.

When Emerald's eggs hatched, the
baby snakes were dark, but they soon
turned green, too.

Emerald liked to eat insects. Stevie
and Jordan both caught caterpillars for

her. But Stevie could tell that Emerald liked him best. When he talked, she listened.

"Emerald, do you like Camp Viper?" Stevie asked.

Emerald's head waved up and down. Stevie was sure that meant "yes."

"Do you wish you were a different color?"

Emerald's head waved back and forth. Stevie was sure that meant "no."

Emerald slithered behind Stevie wherever he went. To baseball games with the other cabins. To pizza parties in the Dining Hall. To visit Emerald's

little green babies in the Ophiolium.

Emerald even followed Stevie to the lake when he went swimming. But she always waited on shore.

Everyone loved Emerald. She was voted the smartest snake at Camp Viper.

Toward the end of the month, Head

Counselor Tim called Stevie over. "I've
been watching you, Stevie. And I'm
very impressed," he said. "I can tell
you really like snakes."

"Yes, sir," Stevie said. "I do."

Stevie wasn't sure if he liked all
snakes yet. But he certainly liked
Emerald. And that was a start.

5
ESCAPE!

A big drop of rain hit Stevie on the head. He looked up. Huge dark clouds covered the sky. Stevie started to run.

He had been helping Tim get ready for Parents' Day. Now all Stevie wanted to do was get in his cabin before it started raining really hard.

He opened the door and stopped.

Jordan was standing in the middle of a group of kids. He was holding Stevie's suitcase.

"Hey! Put that back!" Stevie cried. He raced toward Jordan.

"But it's raining now," Jordan said. "This may be my only chance to study the Horribilis Slimus Vipera."

"I don't care!" Stevie shouted.

There were only a couple of days until the end of camp. Stevie had been so caught up in Emerald, he'd forgotten about the Horribilis Slimus Vipera. Now everyone would know he had just made it up.

He'd probably be kicked out of camp. He didn't want that to happen. He actually liked it at Camp Viper now.

Stevie lunged for his suitcase. But Jordan pulled it away from him and opened it.

It was empty. Everyone gasped.

Stevie bowed his head. Now they knew the truth. Stevie waited for them to start laughing.

Instead, one of the kids cried, "The Horribilis Slimus Vipera has escaped!"

Stevie looked up. "Yes! Yes! That's it!" he shouted. "That must be what happened."

"Hey! Wait a minute!" Jordan said. "Why isn't there green slime all over everything?"

Stevie thought fast. "The Horribilis Slimus Vipera only makes slime during spring and early summer, that's why," he said. "Like when he was crawling all over you."

Jordan shuddered at the memory. "Oh," he said. Then he slumped against the bunk bed. "Now I'll never get to see the rarest snake in the world."

Stevie put his arm around Jordan. "I'm sorry," he said. "But you know more about *other* snakes than anyone."

Stevie smiled. "Besides, the Horribilis Slimus Vipera wasn't much to look at."

"Hey! Maybe it's still in camp," one of the kids shouted. "Let's look for it!"

Jordan jumped up. "That's a great idea. Come on, Stevie!"

Stevie helped search for the rest of the afternoon. Finally, they gave up.

The next day was Parents' Day. The last day of camp.

Stevie was happy to see his mother and father. His mother smothered him with kisses. His father greeted him in Latin.

"I have something to show you," Stevie told them.

When he picked up Emerald, his mother screamed.

When he let Emerald curl around his neck, his father tried to save him.

"Wait, Dad! It's okay!" Stevie said. "Emerald is my friend. She won't hurt me."

Stevie explained to his parents all about his summer, and what he had learned about snakes, and how he'd gotten over being afraid. But his parents still felt bad.

"We're sorry we sent you to the wrong camp," his mother said.

"We must have mixed up the

brochures," his father said.

"I'm glad you did," Stevie said. "I had a great time."

Soon it was time to leave. All the campers gave their snakes to Tim. He'd take care of them at the Regional Snake Sanctuary until next year.

Stevie said good-bye to Emerald. "I'm really going to miss you," he whispered.

He handed Emerald to Tim.

But Tim wouldn't take her. "No, Stevie. Emerald didn't come from the sanctuary. You found her." He gave Stevie a smile. "Besides, her babies are all grown up. I think she'd be happier living with you."

Stevie grinned. He looked at Emerald. She waved her head up and down. He knew that meant "yes."

He turned to his parents. "Okay?"

"Okay," they said reluctantly.

Jordan rushed up to Stevie. "See you next year," he said.

"I'll be here," Stevie said. He told Jordan about Emerald.

"Hey!" Jordan said. "Maybe Ralph and I could visit you and Emerald sometime!"

"That's a great idea!" said Stevie. He

turned to his parents. "Ralph is Jordan's pet bullsnake. He sleeps with Jordan and everything."

Stevie's mother shivered. "I don't know, Stevie."

"Aw, Mom! Snakes aren't bad at all," Stevie said. Emerald wrapped herself around his arm. She hissed in his ear. Stevie met her black eyes. "There's nothing to be afraid of!"